AT THE ORPHANS' DOOR

TOM HIRONS

FERAL ANGELS PRESS

2023

First edition. First printing, 2023
ISBN 978-1-7392170-0-6

Litho-printed on 100% recycled paper by CALVERTS workers' co-op in England.

AT THE ORPHANS' DOOR is set in *Bunyan*

AUTHOR'S NOTE:

Some of these poems have appeared in slightly different forms on social media in the past few years. If there are edits that you notice, I hope that the changes don't feel too disruptive. I sincerely believe that all these pieces are best read aloud. The next book will be called THE QUEEN OF HEAVEN.

T.H.

JUNE 2023

FOR THE EXILES

AND

MY MOTHER

SALLY HIRONS (1941 – 2022)

THESE ARE THE ARROWS I LET LOOSE.

AS I RODE IN DARKNESS,

I AIMED AS TRUE AS I COULD.

CONTENTS

SECRET HEART

Only when you are broken
Will you discover the life
Beneath this life.

Only then can you walk
With your children
And be nowhere
Other than with them.

All your ambition is put aside
For a moment, or a day, or a month.
Those preoccupations you thought
Were your Self are scattered in the wind.
They mean nothing now
And perhaps they never did.

Life has broken you

So that you can kiss
Its terrible, beautiful face.

Now you begin to hear
The beating drum whose pulse
You half-heard all your life.

Now you begin to hear
The secret heart that lives
At the centre of the world.

BLACK MOUNTAIN RIVER

It doesn't take much;
One tug at my feet
By Autumn's grey strangers
And I'm on my way, at last,
Returning.

As if a stream has appeared in front of me
Towards that great Black Mountain of Winter,
Autumn sings me home.

In the womb of Black Mountain,
I'm already waiting,
As patient as a heron
Or the hawthorn on the moor.

Spring's grey sister
Has come for me.

What began with a crocus
Ends with the broken bough,
The leaning-in towards hearth-fire,
The quiet soul-song of the mist
On the black mountainside.

I step into the water,
Leaving Summer's gold and laughter,
Like a man baptised
Into a luminous darkness.

The silver mist closes behind me;
The grey strangers accompany me;
The moon puts pennies on my eyes.

The tragedy of life is not its sadness,
But forgetting the way back home
Along Black Mountain River.

THE NARROW BRIDGE

On the big rowans,
The berries are starting to turn.
The storms have come in and
Summer's been swept away.

In this uncertain moment,
I am threading as best I can
Between love and love's despair,
Through the fear-thick fog, in darkness,
Across a bridge I can barely discern.

I descend, where descent is required,
And ascend on what wings appear before me.
I do not know if my path is righteous,
But it is the only path I see
Which truly bears my name.

All futures shimmer and tremble,
Collapsing towards an unknown fate.
On this slender pathway
I place one foot after the other,
Travelling over the chasm
In the only way I know.

In the hedge behind this cabin,
Where the rowan berries are reddening,
One golden lily is still blooming.
It's an expert only in the art of itself,
As incapable of waning as the sun,
Radiant as its season slides.

I am doing my best,
But it may not be enough.
Each time I pass, I bow to the lily.
As the gales batter us both,
Its beauty and hopeless hope remain.

ORION

In a cold November night, Orion rises
And – for all I know of him – each year,
When those stars appear,
My blood begins to sing.

The stars are not the story,
Or at least this is what I say.
That shape in the dark night,
What is your secret?
Why does my blood sing to you?
How do you lead me home?

Perhaps it's just the turning of the year,
The season's change
And Autumn that reminds me,
But still it is your appearance
As the gathering clouds part

Upon which my hope rides home.

A mystery speaks to me
And the shaped stars sing,
But the words and the song
Are not those I learned in any book.
They are in the language of
The tall stones, a dream-speech;
The spiralled year's tongue.

This is the only telling I'll listen to
As the Winter-dark thickens.
Right or wrong, in my eyes
It lies true against the sky,
Casts no deceitful shadow
On the Earth below.

I call it the starward way
But it is my own Earthly fate

That I hear told in that light.

I lift my eyes to the dark horizon
As the bright stars begin to speak
In that language my ear cannot hold.

My heart grows vast;
I stand to my true height;
The world is a circle around me.

Orion,
I do not understand you,
But, let me speak as true
As the songs you sing
On this November night
In all the language
I cannot hear.

A PARTY FOR THE BROKEN

Tonight we will have a party
Only for the broken pieces.
Only the crooked and the blunt ones
Are welcome tonight;
The shattered and the stained can come,
But you perfected ones should stay away.
All the orphans and exiles
Will be arriving soon with their
Bundles of rags and sorrow.
Make room, you bright angels:
Now the wounded are coming home.

Tonight will be a celebration of our tragedies,
All our petty stupidities,
Our shameful transgressions
And the unedifying failure
To become what we might have been

In other, more radiant lives.

Here are the unrelinquished griefs
And the never-forgiven slights;
Here is the stuttering clumsiness
And all the stagnant laziness.
Here is the hollow in my heart.

Come in.
Welcome.
I'm so glad you're here.

Outside, the Buddhas
And the Saints are laughing.
In here, there is a quieter
Communion of our tragedies.
Sit. There is food and cheap wine,
A warm fire and candles.
Eat. Drink. Then speak,

And we shall all weep
Sticky and graceless tears.

At this party, we are dancing
To ten thousand folksongs.
Each song cracks and falters
And is more darkly holy
For every defective note.

This is the party for the broken.
Imperfect music plays for imperfect dancers.
Imperfect speeches are imperfectly spoken.
We bang tables and forget our words;
We wash the floor with our tears.

You shattered and stained beauties,
All crooked and graceless as you are,
Blunted by the hard world of death,
Love and the push of time's spear;

You who are more glorious than statues,
As rich in stories as pirates,
As worthy as comets or stars,
This is the secret I have
To share with you tonight:

Our dark-tongued singing
Reaches heavens even the Saints don't know;
Our graceless, defiant dancing
Opens up the whole Universe.

Tonight, let the Buddhas be silent;
In here, we will raise our glasses
And sing so loud and badly
That all the bright and dark
Heavens will hear our song.

THE BEDRAGGLED BOYS

I get drunk on good whiskey,
Stand beneath the star-filled sky
And sing my sorrows and joys.

Of scars, I've no more
Or less than most people
Who've lived deep in their lives
And been handed misfortune
As well as great jubilation.

With no great grandeur of wounds,
Only in this explosion of mid-life
Do I at last regard that tapestry,
What animals live in my skin
And what Gods vie on dark
And bright horizons.

I weep now for the boys
And the young men I have been.
Slow to see that the burning blaze
Of my shames were in truth
The beacon fires of my belonging,
I have cloistered myself in caves,
Woven mists and masks
In case I might be seen clearly
As the strange and radiant animal,
The dishevelled angel that I am.

Come home, you bedraggled boys.
The hearth of my heart is warm for you
And my table is set with the best of all I have.
In the mid-light of this late afternoon
I take one step after another
Towards the fires at which you serve.

Look: my arms are strong.

I will carry you close to my heart;
As the twilight gathers,
I will bring your baskets of sorrow
And all your youthful joys
Back to the island of apple trees,
To the feasting hall and
Our everlasting home.

SONGS FOR AN IMPOSSIBLE FUTURE

Look at all this death.
I will plant teeth in the dust and
Water them with my blood
And dry water, with feathers,
With laughter and songs.

When there is nothing left,
I'll pick flowers that grow nowhere
And place them at the doors of dead people.
I'll speak impossible names into the inconsolable
    night,
Sing words for things that don't exist
Or have yet to be born into this world
Of anguish and astonishing love.

I will not be a slave to logic's poverty,
Nor a cog or a brick or a stone.

I was born with wide wings and feet
That stretch for fathoms into the earth.
Everything is extraordinary.

Look at all this death and the lamenting,
The dying, the darkness, the dirge.
I will sing songs for an impossible future
And I will grow a garden out of these bones.

AT MIDSUMMER

In a graveyard in June,
The sun arcs high over
The old parched trees.
Light pours onto the stones.

The skylarks and the blackbirds sing,
Relentless as time's turning.
They have not heard the news.
And would sing their songs, regardless.

I lift my face to the bright horizon
And squint towards rapture or catastrophe,
Or that third thing, which is Life.

I have heard the death-groans of
A thousand of my dreams,
But the life-song of possibility

Still rings loud in my ears.

Here, in love beyond the odds,
Is where I've made my home.
I'll sing and dance all Summer
With death's bridesmaids in the flowers,
Foregoing optimism or despair.

I don't have a choice.
When I turned down death's advances
The decision was made for me.
So, now, I'll make love with this world,
Whether it's in Summer's bright blooming
Or in Winter's wither and the grave.

A CUP OF WONDER

Earth, stars, sea and space
Are all one thing, I say.
But still I cling tight to these old bones
And the stones of my own land,
Prize my children above all others
And cherish this ailing world
Upon whose body I fly
Towards my unknown goal.

Here is the dream-Earth,
Upon whose body I crawl.
This is the dream-Sea,
Across which I carry my
Basket of memory.
These are the dream-Stars,
Beneath whose endless turning
I dance in shadows and light.

Not one of them is unreal
As a dream is unreal;
Not one of them as real
As waking is real.

If you agree that there's no paradox here,
Then stay and drink with me on the veranda.
Tea, wine, water or poetry,
Does it make a difference, or not?

The sunset is exquisite:
Particles of dust and reflected light,
And utterly mysterious wonder.
Witness it with me and let us cry
Into the same cup of wonder,
Before too much knowing
Turns us into talented
And artless fools.

WE FIRE OUR ARROWS IN THE DARK

We are riding a horse bareback at night,
Or at least we think it's a horse. We're not sure.
It's something we've ridden before,
But it still feels new.

We take arrows from a quiver inside our belly
Put them to the bow of our tongue,
Pull back with the muscle of our heart.

Not all of the arrows are straight,
And not all of the straight arrows fly
Better than the ones that are crooked,
Made of ivy-root or stone.

We fire our arrows in the dark
Towards a target we have never seen,
Only sensed with a sense we still have

No certainty we understand.

We will never strike the target.
Yes, this is what I say:
We will never strike the target.

I dance on the precipice of all
That is not possible, with my
Belly full of arrows and my heart
As taut as silence.

But, if one arrow after another
In time flies closer to the target,
Pressing back against the impossible,
Tearing holes in the darkening sky,
My work is done well.

In the immensity of the night
I loose these arrows of possibility,

Hoping always to improve my aim.
With each shudder of the bowstring,
I am shouting *I WILL LOVE THIS ANYWAY*
Into the aching universe.

IN THE MEANTIME

Meanwhile, flowers still bloom.
The moon rises, and the sun.
Babies smile and somewhere,
Against all the odds,
Two people are falling in love.

Strangers share cigarettes and jokes.
Light plays on the surface of water.
Grace occurs on unlikely streets
And we hold each other fast
Against entropy, the fires and the flood.

Life leans towards living
And, while death claims all things at the end,
There were such precious times between,
In which everything was radiant
And we loved, again, this world.

AT THE ORPHANS' DOOR

There is a doorway in the woods
Through which I go sometimes
To gather the scattered people of
My heart's forgotten country.

On the frame of the door
Are scraped the life-marks,
The story-bones of my soul.
Here, I grew taller;
And here I was cut down.
Here, I knew grandeur;
Here, I lost the way.

All the time, I became fuller
And the country richer and thicker,
Than I ever dreamed of,
Both wastes and wonderlands.

Often, I walk past without a look,
Return home, pour food and drink
Into the hole in my heart,
Ignoring the cries of my lost people
And the scent of my soul's own land.
I become thinner by the day.

Beyond the orphans' door,
I exist in all my times and places.
In storms and sweet summers,
I abide in tranquillity and unrest.

Endlessly, I roam the Suffolk woods,
Climb straw-bale castles and
Gather my shame and pride.

Here's a boy with his sweets in a bag
To stuff in stacks into his heart,
A fence against the fracture in his home.

Here's a scrap of a young man,
Long on coffee and short on sleep,
Following a yarn he can hardly hold,
Writing himself into madness or
Out of it on stolen yellow sheets,
Selling his belongings and
Talking to the hedge, in love
With the sparks he makes
As he crosses the dark sky
Or the slate-grey streets of the city.

There's a genius teenager
Making stars spin on a screen
With his words written on the walls,
And a ladder of cuts on his arms
Reaching towards heaven
Or maybe Earth.
In the always-twilight
He takes the blade

To the skin of his face
And moves beyond the world
Into which he was born.
Daylight cannot hold him.

There's me at fourteen and my dead father
Him in his hospital bed, me as numb as I'll ever be,
Standing beside his body
In the grey-forever afternoon
And our frozen family,
Always making that cursed journey
To the hours-away hospital,
Always arriving in the wake
Of his dying and as useless as
A flower for the dead.

In our living room, there's a man
With a knife and sticks,
And junkies in the kitchen, stealing our spoons

And the centre does not hold,
So I'm standing in the corner
And I'm running down the road,
Tripping in the street and
Forever not knowing why
I'm being chased so hard,
Only that I have to run
And keep on running
And keep on. And keep on.

There's twenty-five years of my lost sister;
There's my mother, folding slowly into her
Television set and her theatre of glories,
All our memories of the bright fields long ago;

There's her dancing in the village,
Me six years old, the fairs at Barsham,
Spectacular wonders and pigs in the kitchen;
My jester's hat, my first friend,

Jason Bradley, my sister covered in
Porridge for eczema, the Peppermint Pig
and Scarlet Fever, whatever that was,
And the death of Elvis,
John Lennon being shot forever
And my first kiss,
The way her skin smelled
Of oranges and the ache of
Love found, love lost,
Love and love again.

When I was young,
I believed we were Polish Jews.
I dreamed of barbed wire, over and over,
Machine guns, soldiers at the border
And death hunting us,
Hunting us down.

So, beyond the door there is a boy, a Polish Jew

Boy crouched under an ever-striking hammer.
I don't know his name, but he is also
One of my lost people and I hold him close.

The orphans knock at the door
And each one, every one,
Has a piece of the past
Wrapped in rags and ruin,
A piece of my heart in their
Cut and dusty hands and
Each one's story is a story
I cannot ignore.

I'm too tired of running
And too hungry for my heart.

Come in, I say, *come home.*
And I listen by the fire
Until the tale is told.

These are the scattered people of my heart
Who suffer endlessly or dance in darkness to
The boundless rhythm of time forever stopped.

But, beyond the calamity and confusion
And the shimmering children I've been,
There is a bright figure, dancing,
A man made of gold and light and

Oblivious to the dismay of the world,
Exalting and triumphant as a trumpet,
As nightingales, as daybreak, as eagles
In the sky over the hungry-boned fields.

And by the woods is a man
With the head of a deer,
Forever springing back to the trees,
Forever looking at us across the bright field,
King of that lost country I call home.

THE HIGH WINDOW

The dungeon of hopelessness has twenty-seven
doors.
Twenty-eight old men lie sleeping on their beards
And, once every wretched day,
A hand throws in food through
The high-up, heart-shaped window.

Will you subsist now
On such scant provisions ?
Have you not endured for long enough
On this food of dull survival?
Do not accept such meagre offerings!
Do not eat the rations of mortality!

You live in the palace of miracles now
And wonders of sustenance and courageousness
Are yours to call forth in the darkness.

Do not listen to the old men
Who roll their eyes and intone for you
All the reasons to lie down and die.

Accept nothing less than the miraculous.
You will grow old, too,
Waiting in the dungeon for the fulfilment
Of your half-hearted dreams.

Did you learn nothing
From your long apprenticeship
To misery?

The secret to eternal youth
Is not acceptance of your lot,
But to be bound to your fate
With extraordinary ties of fire.

In the dungeon of twenty seven doors
You'll hear all kinds of woeful gossip.
No one can hold your heart safe
From that persuasive poison.
But, once or twice in your life,
You made a strange ally
And each one had a gift for
This precarious moment.

Spread the cloth; open the casket.
Make a feast for the guests
Whose powers you do not yet know.

That generosity might save your life
And, sometimes, it might save the world.

THE SHAPE OF THINGS

I sing praises now to your uneven shape;
I raise my broken cup to your lopsided soul
And drink deep to the sweet wonder
Of your disorder and disarray.

Don't let the pursuit of balance
Become a mask for a half life safely lived.
You will never be more whole than you are now;
You will never be healed to your satisfaction
Of all the wounds where life's chisel
Carved you into this divine, ungodly form.

Consider this:
You were born to be an arrow
Or a hammer, a falcon in flight, or a key;
A flame, a dance, the shape of a
Kingfisher's wing, a drop of water

On a leaf at dawn or a bell,
A swarm of starlings
Above the sedge at dusk,
Squint, unequal
And perfected.

Balance?
Your soul says only this:
Let me loose.
Let me become my shape.
Stop standing in my way.

Your life could take any number of roads.
This one is tepid and careful and
Beautifully poised.
You can choose it if you like.
And this one is on fire,
It is dangerous. You risk everything.
CHOOSE THIS ROAD.

Surrender to your own shape
And you will be impervious
To five layers of the Gods' curses.
Live life carefully
And you will be subject to the
Ridicule of them all.

In your own shape
You will move through fire
Like it is a river and you
An otter or an eel,
Alive in your most easeful element.

Take the road of your own shape
And you will be worthy of fame,
If only in the invisible sphere
Of your own esteem
And in the holy half-light
Of the world at the orphans' door.